Date: _____ Day: _____ Mood: _____

Intention for the day / week / month / year: _____

MW00897407

Today I am truly grateful for:

_____

_____

_____

My feelings today:

_____

_____

_____

Today's Essentials:

_____

_____

_____

_____

Anything bothering me?

_____

_____

_____

If only...

_____

_____

_____

Today in seven words or less:

_____

_____

Today's Reflections

Date: _____ Day: _____ Mood: _____

Intention for the day / week / month / year: _____

Today I am truly grateful for:

_____

_____

_____

My feelings today:

_____

_____

_____

Today's Essentials:

_____

_____

_____

_____

Anything bothering me?

_____

_____

_____

If only...

_____

_____

_____

Today in seven words or less:

_____

_____

Today's Reflections

Date: _____ Day: _____ Mood: _____

Intention for the day / week / month / year: _____

Today I am truly grateful for:

_____

_____

_____

My feelings today:

_____

_____

_____

Today's Essentials:

_____

_____

_____

_____

Anything bothering me?

_____

_____

If only...

_____

_____

_____

Today in seven words or less:

_____

_____

Today's Reflections

Date: _____ Day: _____ Mood: _____

Intention for the day / week / month / year: _____

Today I am truly grateful for:

_____

_____

_____

My feelings today:

_____

_____

_____

Today's Essentials:

_____

_____

_____

_____

Anything bothering me?

_____

_____

_____

If only...

_____

_____

_____

Today in seven words or less:

_____

_____

Today's Reflections

Date: _____ Day: _____ Mood: _____

Intention for the day / week / month / year: _____

Today I am truly grateful for:

_____

_____

_____

My feelings today:

_____

_____

_____

Today's Essentials:

_____

_____

_____

_____

Anything bothering me?

_____

_____

_____

If only...

_____

_____

_____

Today in seven words or less:

_____

_____

Today's Reflections

Date: _____ Day: _____ Mood: _____

Intention for the day / week / month / year: _____

Today I am truly grateful for:

_____

_____

_____

My feelings today:

_____

_____

_____

Today's Essentials:

_____

_____

_____

_____

Anything bothering me?

_____

_____

_____

If only...

_____

_____

_____

Today in seven words or less:

_____

_____

Today's Reflections

Date: _____ Day: _____ Mood: _____

Intention for the day / week / month / year: _____

Today I am truly grateful for:

_____

_____

_____

My feelings today:

_____

_____

_____

Today's Essentials:

_____

_____

_____

_____

Anything bothering me?

_____

_____

_____

If only...

_____

_____

_____

Today in seven words or less:

_____

_____

Today's Reflections

Date: _____ Day: _____ Mood: _____

Intention for the day / week / month / year: _____

Today I am truly grateful for:

_____

_____

_____

My feelings today:

_____

_____

_____

Today's Essentials:

_____

_____

_____

_____

Anything bothering me?

_____

_____

_____

If only...

_____

_____

_____

Today in seven words or less:

_____

_____

Today's Reflections

Date: _____ Day: _____ Mood: _____

Intention for the day / week / month / year: _____

Today I am truly grateful for:

_____

_____

_____

My feelings today:

_____

_____

_____

Today's Essentials:

_____

_____

_____

_____

Anything bothering me?

_____

_____

_____

If only...

_____

_____

_____

Today in seven words or less:

_____

_____

Today's Reflections

Date: _____ Day: _____ Mood: _____

Intention for the day / week / month / year: _____

Today I am truly grateful for:

_____

_____

_____

My feelings today:

_____

_____

_____

Today's Essentials:

_____

_____

_____

_____

Anything bothering me?

_____

_____

_____

If only...

_____

_____

_____

Today in seven words or less:

_____

_____

Today's Reflections

Date: _____ Day: _____ Mood: _____

Intention for the day / week / month / year: _____

Today I am truly grateful for:

_____

_____

_____

My feelings today:

_____

_____

_____

Today's Essentials:

_____

_____

_____

_____

Anything bothering me?

_____

_____

_____

If only...

_____

_____

_____

Today in seven words or less:

_____

_____

Today's Reflections

Date: _____ Day: _____ Mood: _____

Intention for the day / week / month / year: _____

Today I am truly grateful for:

_____

_____

_____

My feelings today:

_____

_____

_____

Today's Essentials:

_____

_____

_____

_____

Anything bothering me?

_____

_____

_____

If only...

_____

_____

_____

Today in seven words or less:

_____

_____

Today's Reflections

Date: _____ Day: _____ Mood: _____

Intention for the day / week / month / year: _____

Today I am truly grateful for:

_____

_____

_____

My feelings today:

_____

_____

_____

Today's Essentials:

_____

_____

_____

_____

Anything bothering me?

_____

_____

If only...

_____

_____

_____

Today in seven words or less:

_____

_____

Date: _____ Day: _____ Mood: _____

Intention for the day / week / month / year: _____

Today I am truly grateful for:

_____

_____

_____

My feelings today:

_____

_____

_____

Today's Essentials:

_____

_____

_____

_____

Anything bothering me?

_____

_____

_____

If only...

_____

_____

_____

Today in seven words or less:

_____

_____

Today's Reflections

Date: _____ Day: _____ Mood: _____

Intention for the day / week / month / year: _____

Today I am truly grateful for:

_____

_____

_____

My feelings today:

_____

_____

_____

Today's Essentials:

_____

_____

_____

_____

Anything bothering me?

_____

_____

_____

If only...

_____

_____

_____

Today in seven words or less:

_____

_____

Today's Reflections

Date: _____   Day: _____   Mood: _____

Intention for the day / week / month / year: _____

Today I am truly grateful for:

_____

_____

_____

My feelings today:

_____

_____

_____

Today's Essentials:

_____

_____

_____

_____

Anything bothering me?

_____

_____

_____

If only...

_____

_____

_____

Today in seven words or less:

_____

_____

Today's Reflections

Date: _____ Day: _____ Mood: _____

Intention for the day / week / month / year: _____

Today I am truly grateful for:

_____

_____

_____

My feelings today:

_____

_____

_____

Today's Essentials:

_____

_____

_____

_____

Anything bothering me?

_____

_____

_____

If only...

_____

_____

_____

Today in seven words or less:

_____

_____

Today's Reflections

Date: _____ *Day:* _____ *Mood:* _____

Intention for the day / week / month / year: _____

Today I am truly grateful for:

_____

_____

_____

My feelings today:

_____

_____

_____

Today's Essentials:

_____

_____

_____

_____

Anything bothering me?

_____

_____

_____

If only...

_____

_____

_____

Today in seven words or less:

_____

_____

Today's Reflections

Date: _____   Day: _____   Mood: _____

Intention for the day / week / month / year: _____

Today I am truly grateful for:

_____

_____

_____

My feelings today:

_____

_____

_____

Today's Essentials:

_____

_____

_____

_____

Anything bothering me?

_____

_____

_____

If only...

_____

_____

_____

Today in seven words or less:

_____

_____

Today's Reflections

Date: _____   Day: _____   Mood: _____

Intention for the day / week / month / year: _____

Today I am truly grateful for:

_____

_____

_____

My feelings today:

_____

_____

_____

Today's Essentials:

_____

_____

_____

_____

Anything bothering me?

_____

_____

_____

If only...

_____

_____

_____

Today in seven words or less:

_____

_____

Today's Reflections

Date: _____ Day: _____ Mood: _____

Intention for the day / week / month / year: _____

Today I am truly grateful for:

_____

_____

_____

My feelings today:

_____

_____

_____

Today's Essentials:

_____

_____

_____

_____

Anything bothering me?

_____

_____

_____

If only...

_____

_____

_____

Today in seven words or less:

_____

_____

Today's Reflections

Date: _____ Day: _____ Mood: _____

Intention for the day / week / month / year: _____

Today I am truly grateful for:

_____

_____

_____

My feelings today:

_____

_____

_____

Today's Essentials:

_____

_____

_____

Anything bothering me?

_____

_____

_____

If only...

_____

_____

_____

Today in seven words or less:

_____

_____

Today's Reflections

Date: _____ Day: _____ Mood: _____

Intention for the day / week / month / year: _____

Today I am truly grateful for:

_____

_____

_____

My feelings today:

_____

_____

_____

Today's Essentials:

_____

_____

_____

_____

Anything bothering me?

_____

_____

_____

If only...

_____

_____

_____

Today in seven words or less:

_____

_____

Today's Reflections

Date: _____ Day: _____ Mood: _____

Intention for the day / week / month / year: _____

Today I am truly grateful for:

_____

_____

_____

My feelings today:

_____

_____

_____

Today's Essentials:

_____

_____

_____

_____

Anything bothering me?

_____

_____

_____

If only...

_____

_____

_____

Today in seven words or less:

_____

_____

Today's Reflections

Date: _____ Day: _____ Mood: _____

Intention for the day / week / month / year: _____

Today I am truly grateful for:

_____

_____

_____

My feelings today:

_____

_____

_____

Today's Essentials:

_____

_____

_____

_____

Anything bothering me?

_____

_____

_____

If only...

_____

_____

_____

Today in seven words or less:

_____

_____

Today's Reflections

Date: _____ Day: _____ Mood: _____

Intention for the day / week / month / year: _____

Today I am truly grateful for:

_____

_____

_____

My feelings today:

_____

_____

_____

Today's Essentials:

_____

_____

_____

_____

Anything bothering me?

_____

_____

_____

If only...

_____

_____

_____

Today in seven words or less:

_____

_____

Today's Reflections

Date: _____ Day: _____ Mood: _____

Intention for the day / week / month / year: _____

Today I am truly grateful for:

_____

_____

_____

My feelings today:

_____

_____

_____

Today's Essentials:

_____

_____

_____

_____

Anything bothering me?

_____

_____

_____

If only...

_____

_____

_____

Today in seven words or less:

_____

_____

Today's Reflections

Date: _____ Day: _____ Mood: _____

Intention for the day / week / month / year: _____

Today I am truly grateful for:

_____

_____

_____

My feelings today:

_____

_____

_____

Today's Essentials:

_____

_____

_____

_____

Anything bothering me?

_____

_____

_____

If only...

_____

_____

_____

Today in seven words or less:

_____

_____

Today's Reflections

Date: _____ Day: _____ Mood: _____

Intention for the day / week / month / year: _____

Today I am truly grateful for:

_____

_____

_____

My feelings today:

_____

_____

_____

Today's Essentials:

_____

_____

_____

_____

Anything bothering me?

_____

_____

_____

If only...

_____

_____

_____

Today in seven words or less:

_____

_____

Today's Reflections

Date: _____ Day: _____ Mood: _____

Intention for the day / week / month / year: _____

Today I am truly grateful for:

_____

_____

_____

My feelings today:

_____

_____

_____

Today's Essentials:

_____

_____

_____

_____

Anything bothering me?

_____

_____

_____

If only...

_____

_____

_____

Today in seven words or less:

_____

_____

Today's Reflections

Date: _____ Day: _____ Mood: _____

Intention for the day / week / month / year: _____

Today I am truly grateful for:

_____

_____

_____

My feelings today:

_____

_____

_____

Today's Essentials:

_____

_____

_____

_____

Anything bothering me?

_____

_____

_____

If only...

_____

_____

_____

Today in seven words or less:

_____

_____

Today's Reflections

Date: _____ Day: _____ Mood: _____

Intention for the day / week / month / year: _____

Today I am truly grateful for:

_____

_____

_____

My feelings today:

_____

_____

_____

Today's Essentials:

_____

_____

_____

_____

Anything bothering me?

_____

_____

_____

If only...

_____

_____

_____

Today in seven words or less:

_____

_____

Today's Reflections

Date: _____ Day: _____ Mood: _____

Intention for the day / week / month / year: _____

Today I am truly grateful for:

_____

_____

_____

My feelings today:

_____

_____

_____

Today's Essentials:

_____

_____

_____

_____

Anything bothering me?

_____

_____

_____

If only...

_____

_____

_____

Today in seven words or less:

_____

_____

Today's Reflections

Date: _____ Day: _____ Mood: _____

Intention for the day / week / month / year: _____

Today I am truly grateful for:

_____

_____

_____

My feelings today:

_____

_____

_____

Today's Essentials:

_____

_____

_____

_____

Anything bothering me?

_____

_____

_____

If only...

_____

_____

_____

Today in seven words or less:

_____

_____

Today's Reflections

Date: _____ Day: _____ Mood: _____

Intention for the day / week / month / year: _____

Today I am truly grateful for:

_____

_____

_____

My feelings today:

_____

_____

_____

Today's Essentials:

_____

_____

_____

_____

Anything bothering me?

_____

_____

_____

If only...

_____

_____

_____

Today in seven words or less:

_____

_____

Today's Reflections

Date: _____ Day: _____ Mood: _____

Intention for the day / week / month / year: _____

Today I am truly grateful for:

_____

_____

_____

My feelings today:

_____

_____

_____

Today's Essentials:

_____

_____

_____

_____

Anything bothering me?

_____

_____

_____

If only...

_____

_____

_____

Today in seven words or less:

_____

_____

Today's Reflections

Date: _____ Day: _____ Mood: _____

Intention for the day / week / month / year: _____

Today I am truly grateful for:

_____

_____

_____

My feelings today:

_____

_____

_____

Today's Essentials:

_____

_____

_____

_____

Anything bothering me?

_____

_____

_____

If only...

_____

_____

_____

Today in seven words or less:

_____

_____

Today's Reflections

Date: _____ Day: _____ Mood: _____

Intention for the day / week / month / year: _____

Today I am truly grateful for:

_____

_____

_____

My feelings today:

_____

_____

_____

Today's Essentials:

_____

_____

_____

_____

Anything bothering me?

_____

_____

_____

If only...

_____

_____

_____

Today in seven words or less:

_____

_____

Today's Reflections

Date: _____ Day: _____ Mood: _____

Intention for the day / week / month / year: _____

Today I am truly grateful for:

_____

_____

_____

My feelings today:

_____

_____

_____

Today's Essentials:

_____

_____

_____

_____

Anything bothering me?

_____

_____

_____

If only...

_____

_____

_____

Today in seven words or less:

_____

_____

Today's Reflections

Date: _____ Day: _____ Mood: _____

Intention for the day / week / month / year: _____

Today I am truly grateful for:

_____

_____

_____

My feelings today:

_____

_____

_____

Today's Essentials:

_____

_____

_____

_____

Anything bothering me?

_____

_____

_____

If only...

_____

_____

_____

Today in seven words or less:

_____

_____

Today's Reflections

Date: _____ Day: _____ Mood: _____

Intention for the day / week / month / year: _____

Today I am truly grateful for:

_____

_____

_____

My feelings today:

_____

_____

_____

Today's Essentials:

_____

_____

_____

_____

Anything bothering me?

_____

_____

_____

If only...

_____

_____

_____

Today in seven words or less:

_____

_____

Today's Reflections

Date: _____ Day: _____ Mood: _____

Intention for the day / week / month / year: _____

Today I am truly grateful for:

_____

_____

_____

My feelings today:

_____

_____

_____

Today's Essentials:

_____

_____

_____

Anything bothering me?

_____

_____

_____

If only...

_____

_____

_____

Today in seven words or less:

_____

_____

Today's Reflections

Date: _____ Day: _____ Mood: _____

Intention for the day / week / month / year: _____

Today I am truly grateful for:

_____

_____

_____

My feelings today:

_____

_____

_____

Today's Essentials:

_____

_____

_____

_____

Anything bothering me?

_____

_____

_____

If only...

_____

_____

_____

Today in seven words or less:

_____

_____

Today's Reflections

Date: _____ Day: _____ Mood: _____

Intention for the day / week / month / year: _____

Today I am truly grateful for:

_____

_____

_____

My feelings today:

_____

_____

_____

Today's Essentials:

_____

_____

_____

_____

Anything bothering me?

_____

_____

_____

If only...

_____

_____

_____

Today in seven words or less:

_____

_____

Today's Reflections

Date: _____ Day: _____ Mood: _____

Intention for the day / week / month / year: _____

Today I am truly grateful for:

_____

_____

_____

My feelings today:

_____

_____

_____

Today's Essentials:

_____

_____

_____

_____

Anything bothering me?

_____

_____

_____

If only...

_____

_____

_____

Today in seven words or less:

_____

_____

Today's Reflections

Date: _____ Day: _____ Mood: _____

Intention for the day / week / month / year: _____

Today I am truly grateful for:

_____

_____

_____

My feelings today:

_____

_____

_____

Today's Essentials:

_____

_____

_____

_____

Anything bothering me?

_____

_____

_____

If only...

_____

_____

_____

Today in seven words or less:

_____

_____

Today's Reflections

Date: _____   Day: _____   Mood: _____

Intention for the day / week / month / year: _____

Today I am truly grateful for:

_____

_____

_____

My feelings today:

_____

_____

_____

Today's Essentials:

_____

_____

_____

_____

Anything bothering me?

_____

_____

_____

If only...

_____

_____

_____

Today in seven words or less:

_____

_____

Date: _____   Day: _____   Mood: _____

Intention for the day / week / month / year: _____

Today I am truly grateful for:

_____

_____

_____

My feelings today:

_____

_____

_____

Today's Essentials:

_____

_____

_____

_____

Anything bothering me?

_____

_____

If only...

_____

_____

_____

Today in seven words or less:

_____

_____

Today's Reflections

Date: _____ Day: _____ Mood: _____

Intention for the day / week / month / year: _____

Today I am truly grateful for:

_____

_____

_____

My feelings today:

_____

_____

_____

Today's Essentials:

_____

_____

_____

_____

Anything bothering me?

_____

_____

_____

If only...

_____

_____

_____

Today in seven words or less:

_____

_____

Today's Reflections

Date: _____ Day: _____ Mood: _____

Intention for the day / week / month / year: _____

Today I am truly grateful for:

_____

_____

_____

My feelings today:

_____

_____

_____

Today's Essentials:

_____

_____

_____

_____

Anything bothering me?

_____

_____

_____

If only...

_____

_____

_____

Today in seven words or less:

_____

_____

Today's Reflections

Date: _____   Day: _____   Mood: _____

Intention for the day / week / month / year: _____

Today I am truly grateful for:

_____

_____

_____

My feelings today:

_____

_____

_____

Today's Essentials:

_____

_____

_____

_____

Anything bothering me?

_____

_____

_____

If only...

_____

_____

_____

Today in seven words or less:

_____

_____

Today's Reflections

Date: _____ Day: _____ Mood: _____

Intention for the day / week / month / year: _____

Today I am truly grateful for:

_____

_____

_____

My feelings today:

_____

_____

_____

Today's Essentials:

_____

_____

_____

_____

Anything bothering me?

_____

_____

_____

If only...

_____

_____

_____

Today in seven words or less:

_____

_____

Today's Reflections

Date: _____ Day: _____ Mood: _____

Intention for the day / week / month / year: _____

Today I am truly grateful for:

_____

_____

_____

My feelings today:

_____

_____

_____

Today's Essentials:

_____

_____

_____

_____

Anything bothering me?

_____

_____

_____

If only...

_____

_____

_____

Today in seven words or less:

_____

_____

Today's Reflections

Date: _____ Day: _____ Mood: _____

Intention for the day / week / month / year: _____

Today I am truly grateful for:

_____

_____

_____

My feelings today:

_____

_____

_____

Today's Essentials:

_____

_____

_____

_____

Anything bothering me?

_____

_____

If only...

_____

_____

_____

Today in seven words or less:

_____

_____

Today's Reflections

Date: _____ Day: _____ Mood: _____

Intention for the day / week / month / year: _____

Today I am truly grateful for:

_____

_____

_____

My feelings today:

_____

_____

_____

Today's Essentials:

_____

_____

_____

_____

Anything bothering me?

_____

_____

_____

If only...

_____

_____

_____

Today in seven words or less:

_____

_____

Today's Reflections

Date: _____ Day: _____ Mood: _____

Intention for the day / week / month / year: _____

Today I am truly grateful for:

_____

_____

_____

My feelings today:

_____

_____

_____

Today's Essentials:

_____

_____

_____

_____

Anything bothering me?

_____

_____

_____

If only...

_____

_____

_____

Today in seven words or less:

_____

_____

Today's Reflections

Date: _____ Day: _____ Mood: _____

Intention for the day / week / month / year: _____

Today I am truly grateful for:

_____

_____

_____

My feelings today:

_____

_____

_____

Today's Essentials:

_____

_____

_____

_____

Anything bothering me?

_____

_____

_____

If only...

_____

_____

_____

Today in seven words or less:

_____

_____

Today's Reflections

Date: _____ Day: _____ Mood: _____

Intention for the day / week / month / year: _____

Today I am truly grateful for:

_____

_____

_____

My feelings today:

_____

_____

_____

Today's Essentials:

_____

_____

_____

_____

Anything bothering me?

_____

_____

_____

If only...

_____

_____

_____

Today in seven words or less:

_____

_____

Today's Reflections

Date: _____   Day: _____   Mood: _____

Intention for the day / week / month / year: _____

Today I am truly grateful for:

_____

_____

_____

My feelings today:

_____

_____

_____

Today's Essentials:

_____

_____

_____

_____

Anything bothering me?

_____

_____

_____

If only...

_____

_____

_____

Today in seven words or less:

_____

_____

Today's Reflections

Date: _____ Day: _____ Mood: _____

Intention for the day / week / month / year: _____

Today I am truly grateful for:

_____

_____

_____

My feelings today:

_____

_____

_____

Today's Essentials:

_____

_____

_____

_____

Anything bothering me?

_____

_____

_____

If only...

_____

_____

_____

Today in seven words or less:

_____

_____

Today's Reflections

Date: _____ Day: _____ Mood: _____

Intention for the day / week / month / year: _____

Today I am truly grateful for:

_____

_____

_____

My feelings today:

_____

_____

_____

Today's Essentials:

_____

_____

_____

_____

Anything bothering me?

_____

_____

_____

If only...

_____

_____

_____

Today in seven words or less:

_____

_____

Today's Reflections

Date: _____ Day: _____ Mood: _____

Intention for the day / week / month / year: _____

Today I am truly grateful for:

_____

_____

_____

My feelings today:

_____

_____

_____

Today's Essentials:

_____

_____

_____

_____

Anything bothering me?

_____

_____

_____

If only...

_____

_____

_____

Today in seven words or less:

_____

_____

Today's Reflections

Date: _____   Day: _____   Mood: _____

Intention for the day / week / month / year: _____

Today I am truly grateful for:

_____

_____

_____

My feelings today:

_____

_____

_____

Today's Essentials:

_____

_____

_____

_____

Anything bothering me?

_____

_____

_____

If only...

_____

_____

_____

Today in seven words or less:

_____

_____

Today's Reflections

Date: _____   Day: _____   Mood: _____

Intention for the day / week / month / year: _____

Today I am truly grateful for:

_____

_____

_____

My feelings today:

_____

_____

_____

Today's Essentials:

_____

_____

_____

_____

Anything bothering me?

_____

_____

_____

If only...

_____

_____

_____

Today in seven words or less:

_____

_____

Today's Reflections

Date: _____ Day: _____ Mood: _____

Intention for the day / week / month / year: _____

Today I am truly grateful for:

_____

_____

_____

My feelings today:

_____

_____

_____

Today's Essentials:

_____

_____

_____

_____

Anything bothering me?

_____

_____

_____

If only...

_____

_____

_____

Today in seven words or less:

_____

_____

Today's Reflections

Date: _____ Day: _____ Mood: _____

Intention for the day / week / month / year: _____

Today I am truly grateful for:

_____

_____

_____

My feelings today:

_____

_____

_____

Today's Essentials:

_____

_____

_____

_____

Anything bothering me?

_____

_____

_____

If only...

_____

_____

_____

Today in seven words or less:

_____

_____

Today's Reflections

Date: _____ Day: _____ Mood: _____

Intention for the day / week / month / year: _____

Today I am truly grateful for:

_____

_____

_____

My feelings today:

_____

_____

_____

Today's Essentials:

_____

_____

_____

_____

Anything bothering me?

_____

_____

_____

If only...

_____

_____

_____

Today in seven words or less:

_____

_____

Today's Reflections

Date: _____ Day: _____ Mood: _____

Intention for the day / week / month / year: _____

Today I am truly grateful for:

_____

_____

_____

My feelings today:

_____

_____

_____

Today's Essentials:

_____

_____

_____

_____

Anything bothering me?

_____

_____

_____

If only...

_____

_____

_____

Today in seven words or less:

_____

_____

Today's Reflections

Date: _____ Day: _____ Mood: _____

Intention for the day / week / month / year: _____

Today I am truly grateful for:

_____

_____

_____

My feelings today:

_____

_____

_____

Today's Essentials:

_____

_____

_____

_____

Anything bothering me?

_____

_____

_____

If only...

_____

_____

_____

Today in seven words or less:

_____

_____

Today's Reflections

Date: _____ Day: _____ Mood: _____

Intention for the day / week / month / year: _____

Today I am truly grateful for:

_____

_____

_____

My feelings today:

_____

_____

_____

Today's Essentials:

_____

_____

_____

_____

Anything bothering me?

_____

_____

_____

If only...

_____

_____

_____

Today in seven words or less:

_____

_____

Today's Reflections

Date: _____ *Day:* _____ *Mood:* _____

Intention for the day / week / month / year: _____

Today I am truly grateful for:

_____

_____

_____

My feelings today:

_____

_____

_____

Today's Essentials:

_____

_____

_____

_____

Anything bothering me?

_____

_____

_____

If only...

_____

_____

_____

Today in seven words or less:

_____

_____

Today's Reflections

Date: _____ Day: _____ Mood: _____

Intention for the day / week / month / year: _____

Today I am truly grateful for:

_____

_____

_____

My feelings today:

_____

_____

_____

Today's Essentials:

_____

_____

_____

_____

Anything bothering me?

_____

_____

_____

If only...

_____

_____

_____

Today in seven words or less:

_____

_____

Today's Reflections

Date: _____ Day: _____ Mood: _____

Intention for the day / week / month / year: _____

Today I am truly grateful for:

_____

_____

_____

My feelings today:

_____

_____

_____

Today's Essentials:

_____

_____

_____

_____

Anything bothering me?

_____

_____

_____

If only...

_____

_____

_____

Today in seven words or less:

_____

_____

Today's Reflections

Date: _____ Day: _____ Mood: _____

Intention for the day / week / month / year: _____

Today I am truly grateful for:

_____

_____

_____

My feelings today:

_____

_____

_____

Today's Essentials:

_____

_____

_____

_____

Anything bothering me?

_____

_____

_____

If only...

_____

_____

_____

Today in seven words or less:

_____

_____

Today's Reflections

Date: _____ Day: _____ Mood: _____

Intention for the day / week / month / year: _____

Today I am truly grateful for:

_____

_____

_____

My feelings today:

_____

_____

_____

Today's Essentials:

_____

_____

_____

_____

Anything bothering me?

_____

_____

_____

If only...

_____

_____

_____

Today in seven words or less:

_____

_____

Today's Reflections

Date: _____ Day: _____ Mood: _____

Intention for the day / week / month / year: _____

Today I am truly grateful for:

_____

_____

_____

My feelings today:

_____

_____

_____

Today's Essentials:

_____

_____

_____

_____

Anything bothering me?

_____

_____

_____

If only...

_____

_____

_____

Today in seven words or less:

_____

_____

Today's Reflections

Date: _____ Day: _____ Mood: _____

Intention for the day / week / month / year: _____

Today I am truly grateful for:

_____

_____

_____

My feelings today:

_____

_____

_____

Today's Essentials:

_____

_____

_____

_____

Anything bothering me?

_____

_____

_____

If only...

_____

_____

_____

Today in seven words or less:

_____

_____

Today's Reflections

Date: _____ Day: _____ Mood: _____

Intention for the day / week / month / year: _____

Today I am truly grateful for:

_____

_____

_____

My feelings today:

_____

_____

_____

Today's Essentials:

_____

_____

_____

_____

Anything bothering me?

_____

_____

_____

If only...

_____

_____

_____

Today in seven words or less:

_____

_____

Today's Reflections

Date: _____   Day: _____   Mood: _____

Intention for the day / week / month / year: _____

Today I am truly grateful for:

_____

_____

_____

My feelings today:

_____

_____

_____

Today's Essentials:

_____

_____

_____

_____

Anything bothering me?

_____

_____

_____

If only...

_____

_____

_____

Today in seven words or less:

_____

_____

Today's Reflections

Date: _____   Day: _____   Mood: _____

Intention for the day / week / month / year: _____

Today I am truly grateful for:

_____

_____

_____

My feelings today:

_____

_____

_____

Today's Essentials:

_____

_____

_____

_____

Anything bothering me?

_____

_____

_____

If only...

_____

_____

_____

Today in seven words or less:

_____

_____

Today's Reflections

Date: _____   Day: _____   Mood: _____

Intention for the day / week / month / year: _____

Today I am truly grateful for:

_____

_____

_____

My feelings today:

_____

_____

_____

Today's Essentials:

_____

_____

_____

_____

Anything bothering me?

_____

_____

_____

If only...

_____

_____

_____

Today in seven words or less:

_____

_____

Today's Reflections

Date: _____ Day: _____ Mood: _____

Intention for the day / week / month / year: _____

Today I am truly grateful for:

_____

_____

_____

My feelings today:

_____

_____

_____

Today's Essentials:

_____

_____

_____

_____

Anything bothering me?

_____

_____

_____

If only...

_____

_____

_____

Today in seven words or less:

_____

_____

Today's Reflections

Date: _____   *Day:* _____   *Mood:* _____

Intention for the day / week / month / year: _____

Today I am truly grateful for:

_____

_____

_____

My feelings today:

_____

_____

_____

Today's Essentials:

_____

_____

_____

_____

Anything bothering me?

_____

_____

_____

If only...

_____

_____

_____

Today in seven words or less:

_____

_____

Today's Reflections

Date: _____   Day: _____   Mood: _____

Intention for the day / week / month / year: _____

Today I am truly grateful for:

_____

_____

_____

My feelings today:

_____

_____

_____

Today's Essentials:

_____

_____

_____

Anything bothering me?

_____

_____

_____

If only...

_____

_____

_____

Today in seven words or less:

_____

_____

Today's Reflections

Date: _____ Day: _____ Mood: _____

Intention for the day / week / month / year: _____

Today I am truly grateful for:

_____

_____

_____

My feelings today:

_____

_____

_____

Today's Essentials:

_____

_____

_____

_____

Anything bothering me?

_____

_____

_____

If only...

_____

_____

_____

Today in seven words or less:

_____

_____

Today's Reflections

174

Date: _____ Day: _____ Mood: _____

Intention for the day / week / month / year: _____

Today I am truly grateful for:

_____

_____

_____

My feelings today:

_____

_____

_____

Today's Essentials:

_____

_____

_____

_____

Anything bothering me?

_____

_____

_____

If only...

_____

_____

_____

Today in seven words or less:

_____

_____

Today's Reflections

Date: _____ Day: _____ Mood: _____

Intention for the day / week / month / year: _____

Today I am truly grateful for:

_____

_____

_____

My feelings today:

_____

_____

_____

Today's Essentials:

_____

_____

_____

_____

Anything bothering me?

_____

_____

_____

If only...

_____

_____

_____

Today in seven words or less:

_____

_____

Today's Reflections

Date: _____ Day: _____ Mood: _____

Intention for the day / week / month / year: _____

Today I am truly grateful for:

_____

_____

_____

My feelings today:

_____

_____

_____

Today's Essentials:

_____

_____

_____

_____

Anything bothering me?

_____

_____

_____

If only...

_____

_____

_____

Today in seven words or less:

_____

_____

Today's Reflections

Date: _____ Day: _____ Mood: _____

Intention for the day / week / month / year: _____

Today I am truly grateful for:

_____

_____

_____

My feelings today:

_____

_____

_____

Today's Essentials:

_____

_____

_____

_____

Anything bothering me?

_____

_____

_____

If only...

_____

_____

_____

Today in seven words or less:

_____

_____

Today's Reflections

Date: _____   Day: _____   Mood: _____

Intention for the day / week / month / year: _____

Today I am truly grateful for:

_____

_____

_____

My feelings today:

_____

_____

_____

Today's Essentials:

_____

_____

_____

_____

Anything bothering me?

_____

_____

_____

If only...

_____

_____

_____

Today in seven words or less:

_____

_____

Today's Reflections

Date: _____   Day: _____   Mood: _____

Intention for the day / week / month / year: _____

Today I am truly grateful for:

_____

_____

_____

My feelings today:

_____

_____

_____

Today's Essentials:

_____

_____

_____

_____

Anything bothering me?

_____

_____

_____

If only...

_____

_____

_____

Today in seven words or less:

_____

_____

Today's Reflections

Date: _____ Day: _____ Mood: _____

Intention for the day / week / month / year: _____

Today I am truly grateful for:

_____

_____

_____

My feelings today:

_____

_____

_____

Today's Essentials:

_____

_____

_____

_____

Anything bothering me?

_____

_____

_____

If only...

_____

_____

_____

Today in seven words or less:

_____

_____

Today's Reflections

Date: _____   Day: _____   Mood: _____

Intention for the day / week / month / year: _____

Today I am truly grateful for:

_____

_____

_____

My feelings today:

_____

_____

_____

Today's Essentials:

_____

_____

_____

_____

Anything bothering me?

_____

_____

_____

If only...

_____

_____

_____

Today in seven words or less:

_____

_____

Today's Reflections

Date: _____   Day: _____   Mood: _____

Intention for the day / week / month / year: _____

Today I am truly grateful for:

_____

_____

_____

My feelings today:

_____

_____

_____

Today's Essentials:

_____

_____

_____

_____

Anything bothering me?

_____

_____

_____

If only...

_____

_____

_____

Today in seven words or less:

_____

_____

Today's Reflections

Date: _____ Day: _____ Mood: _____

Intention for the day / week / month / year: _____

Today I am truly grateful for:

_____

_____

_____

My feelings today:

_____

_____

_____

Today's Essentials:

_____

_____

_____

_____

Anything bothering me?

_____

_____

_____

If only...

_____

_____

_____

Today in seven words or less:

_____

_____

Today's Reflections

Date: _____   Day: _____   Mood: _____

Intention for the day / week / month / year: _____

Today I am truly grateful for:

_____

_____

_____

My feelings today:

_____

_____

_____

Today's Essentials:

_____

_____

_____

_____

Anything bothering me?

_____

_____

_____

If only...

_____

_____

_____

Today in seven words or less:

_____

_____

Today's Reflections

Date: _____ Day: _____ Mood: _____

Intention for the day / week / month / year: _____

Today I am truly grateful for:

_____

_____

_____

My feelings today:

_____

_____

_____

Today's Essentials:

_____

_____

_____

_____

Anything bothering me?

_____

_____

_____

If only...

_____

_____

_____

Today in seven words or less:

_____

_____

Today's Reflections

Date: _____ Day: _____ Mood: _____

Intention for the day / week / month / year: _____

Today I am truly grateful for:

_____

_____

_____

My feelings today:

_____

_____

_____

Today's Essentials:

_____

_____

_____

_____

Anything bothering me?

_____

_____

_____

If only...

_____

_____

_____

Today in seven words or less:

_____

_____

Today's Reflections

Date: _____ Day: _____ Mood: _____

Intention for the day / week / month / year: _____

Today I am truly grateful for:

_____

_____

_____

My feelings today:

_____

_____

_____

Today's Essentials:

_____

_____

_____

_____

Anything bothering me?

_____

_____

_____

If only...

_____

_____

_____

Today in seven words or less:

_____

_____

Final Reflections

45506426R00114

Made in the USA
Middletown, DE
06 July 2017